CHIZI'S TALE

The True Story of an Orphaned Black Rhino

WRITTEN BY **Jack Jones**   ILLUSTRATED BY **Jacqui Taylor**

KERAS

GREENWICH, CT

ON A HOT August day in Zimbabwe, for reasons we will never know, a baby black rhino got separated from its mother. It was only one day old.

By the time two park rangers found
the baby black rhino, it was very sick.

The rangers called the manager of the local
national park. His name was Colin Saxon.
Colin knew that if the baby black rhino were
left on its own, it would either starve or die
of thirst or maybe even be attacked by a
lion. It *was* Africa, after all.

So Colin took the baby black rhino home to his family. His wife was named Abby, and his children were Angie, Cody, and Jonah. The little rhino would grow up to be one of the biggest and fiercest animals in Africa, but for now it was a new family pet.

The tiny rhino was a boy, and they named him Chisiwana, which means "Orphaned One" in the language people speak in Zimbabwe. The children gave him the nickname Chizi.

Chizi may have been a baby, but he sure ate a lot.
Chizi may have been a baby, but he sure peed a lot.
Whenever he bent his legs a certain way, it meant
he had to pee and someone had to run for a bucket.
Sometimes they got to Chizi in time...

and sometimes

they didn't...

Because Chizi was a baby, he was scared of many
things. He was scared of the dark and liked to
suck on someone's thumb to calm himself down.
He was scared of loud noises, too. They made him
run and hide behind a tree.

Chizi loved to roll around in the mud, butt his
head against a swinging tire, and play soccer.
It was good thing his horn wasn't very big yet.

Chizi really loved taking naps under the air conditioner inside the Saxon house. Sometimes, the only way to get him back outside was to bribe him with a cookie or a banana.

Chizi didn't love it when the kids dressed him up like a unicorn. He would shake off the shiny purple cloak as if it were on fire.

Chizi really didn't love being rushed
on afternoon walks. Sometimes the
family would hide behind a rock,
making Chizi think he was alone.

That would scare him and he would squeal and run full speed ahead with his tail curled like a pig's. The family didn't like playing this trick on Chizi, but it did pick up his pace.

The children did lots
of things with Chizi and found
him very useful. When the children
did their homework, they used Chizi
as a desk. When the children took
a nap, they used Chizi
as a pillow.

And once, when the
children played baseball,
they used Chizi in the outfield.
He wasn't very good.

Like all children, Chizi could be very mischievous. On really hot days, he would sneak into the Saxon family shower and wiggle his back to turn on the water.

One time in the shower, he accidentally got
Jonah's underwear wrapped around his horn.
It put Chizi in a tizzy and gave him a fright.

As Chizi grew older and bigger, Colin took him on trips back into the wild so he could learn his way.

Chizi learned how to eat twigs and branches, how to climb rocks, and how to be with other wild animals.

One day Chizi spotted
another black rhino and
stared at it for a long time.

When Chizi turns three, Colin will release him back into the wild because he will be able to live by himself. It will be a sad day for the Saxon family but an exciting adventure for Chizi.

Colin will leave Chizi to become independent,
just like his mother would have.

All black rhino mothers leave their babies once
they are old enough to take care of themselves.
Those baby black rhinos live alone, happy, and free,
and one day have baby black rhinos of their own.

Tusk

www.tusk.org

Tusk has been actively supporting wildlife, communities, and education in Africa since 1990, investing over $36 million into a broad range of conservation programs. The charity funds over 50 projects across 18 countries, and its environmental education program, PACE, is now promoted in 26 nations.

Tusk believes that the future of Africa's natural world is dependent on improving education for its people, as well as providing protection for its precious wildlife. So Tusk also helps to fund the construction and equipment of primary and secondary schools, as well as installing clean water projects in remote areas.

The charity's work includes the protection of endangered African species ranging from the majestic elephant to the gentle sea turtle.

Tusk is currently working hard to halt the illegal wildlife trade in elephant ivory and rhino horn. The survival of the rhino is threatened by the demand for its horn from buyers in the Far East. Unfortunately, some people believe that powdered rhino horn will cure them of various illnesses. This is not true: The horn is made of keratin, like our fingernails, and does not cure any sicknesses.

The black rhino is now listed as "critically endangered," with approximately 4,800 left in the wild in Africa. The white rhino is classed as "endangered," with approximately 20,000 remaining.

With your support and the help of many others around the world, including Tusk's Royal Patron, Prince William, the Duke of Cambridge, Tusk aims to turn the tide. If poaching continues, this ancient species, which has existed on our planet for 40 million years, faces the very real prospect of extinction in our lifetime. We cannot be the generation that allows this to happen.

The charity has offices in the UK and USA. Please visit our website and do everything you can to support Tusk's work.

TUSK TRUST

4 Cheapside House, High Street
Gillingham, Dorset SP8 4AA, UK
Tel: +44 1747 831005
Fax: +44 1747 831006
Email: info@tusk.org

UK Registered Charity No 803118

TUSK USA

525 East 89th Street
New York, NY 10128
Tel: 212 602 1588
Email: infousa@tusk.org

Tusk USA is a 501(c)(3) nonprofit organization.
EIN 30-0190986

TUSK ONLINE

Website: www.tusk.org
Facebook: www.facebook.com/tusktrust
Twitter: @TUSKTRUST

100% OF THE PROCEEDS FROM THIS BOOK WILL BENEFIT TUSK IN ITS WORK TO SAVE THE BLACK RHINO.

PROTECTING WILDLIFE - SUPPORTING COMMUNITIES - PROMOTING EDUCATION

TEN RHINO FACTS

1.   Chizi is a black rhinoceros, but there are five species of rhinos across the world: The black rhino and white rhino live in Africa, while the Javan rhino, the Sumatran rhino, and the great one-horned rhino live in Asia. The Javan rhino is now almost extinct, with fewer than 50 animals surviving.

2.   Strangely, both the black rhino and the white rhino are actually gray, and the main difference between them is their lips. Black rhinos have pointed upper lips so they can eat bushes and small branches. *Browse* is a word sometimes used to describe twigs and branches, so a black rhino is called a *browser*. White rhinos, meanwhile, have square lips because they prefer to eat grass, and that's why they're *grazers*.

3.   In 1970, there were approximately 65,000 black rhinos in Africa. By 1993, that number had crashed to 2,300 living in the wild. Because of anti-poaching efforts, the number has climbed back to a little over 4,800 today.

4.   Black rhinos can live to be 35 years old in the wild and over 45 years old in captivity.

5.   Black rhinos can end up weighing over 3,000 pounds, and they gain all of that weight from eating just plants.

6.   An animal that eats just plants is called an *herbivore*. An animal that eats meat is called a *carnivore*. An animal that eats both meat and plants is called an *omnivore*.

7.   The black rhino has two horns: one on the front of its long nose and one just a little behind it. The one in front is bigger and has been known to grow up to five feet long.

8.   Those horns are the reason black rhinos are being killed in such large numbers. People in China, Taiwan, Hong Kong, Vietnam, and Singapore believe the horns of a black rhino contain special powerful medicines. However, the scientific truth is that their horns have no medicinal value whatsoever, because they are made of keratin, which is the same stuff that human fingernails are made of.

9.   Black rhinos are also being killed for people in Middle Eastern countries like Yemen or Saudi Arabia who value their horns as expensive ornaments. The market price for a rhino horn now makes it more valuable than gold.

10. It is illegal to hunt black rhinos, but because their horns are so valuable, some hunters take the risk. People who hunt illegally are called *poachers*.

COOL BONUS FACT

11. A group of rhinos is actually called a *crash*.

For my loving parents, Paul and Sonia

Text by Jack Jones
Illustrations by Jacqui Taylor

Book designed by Kirk Benshoff

Keras Publishing
c/o Jones Family Office
One American Lane
Greenwich, CT 06831

Visit our website at www.chizistale.com

First Edition: September 2014

ISBN: 978-0-692-22042-9

10 9 8 7 6 5 4 3 2 1

PHX

Printed in the United States of America